W9-CCA-937

DIG
WAIT
LISTEN

A DESERT TOAD'S TALE

BY **APRIL PULLEY SAYRE**
PICTURES BY **BARBARA BASH**

GREENWILLOW BOOKS
An Imprint of HarperCollinsPublishers

 **D**eep in the desert, under the sand, the spadefoot toad waits. She waits . . . for the sound of rain.

Skitter, skitter, scratch.

She hears soft sounds.

Is this the rain at last?

No. It's a scorpion overhead,

crawling slowly past.

Skitter, scratch!

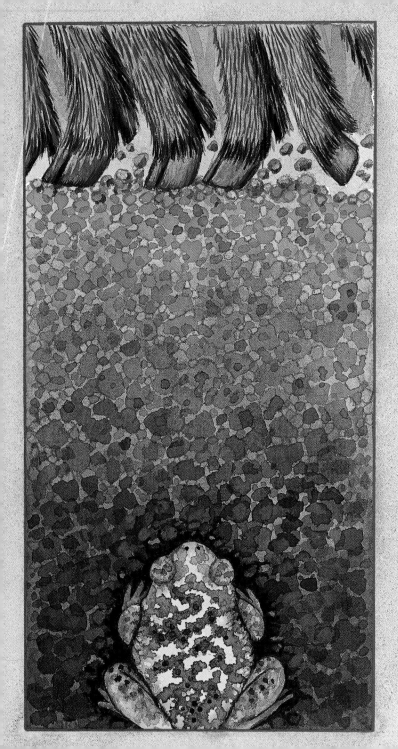

Thunk, thunk, thunk.
Clink, clunk,
clink, clunk.

Sounds shake the soil.

But it's only a herd of peccaries.

Their hooves hammer the ground.

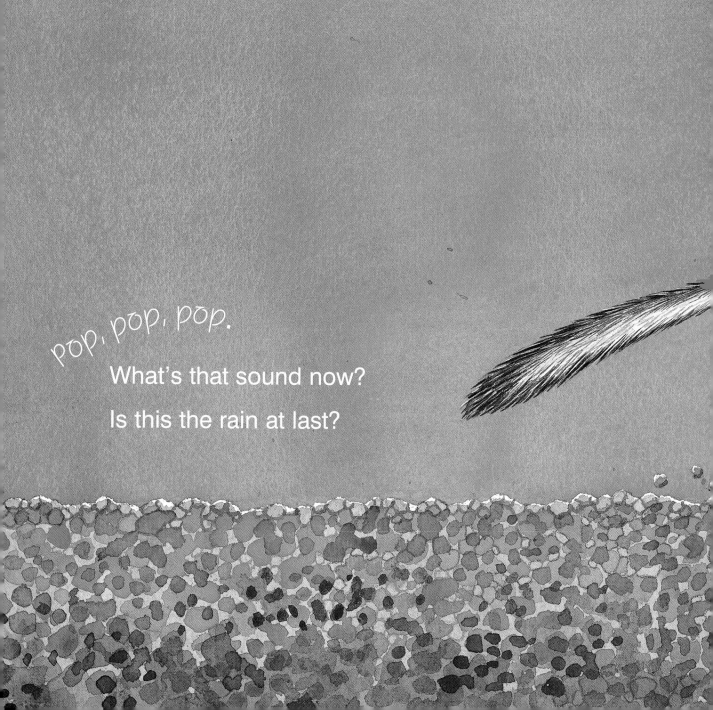

pop, pop, pop.

What's that sound now?

Is this the rain at last?

No, it's a rat,

hopping in lengthy leaps

like a tiny kangaroo.

Will the rain *ever* come?

The desert's so hot, so dry!

And the toad's been waiting

so many months

in her basement burrow home.

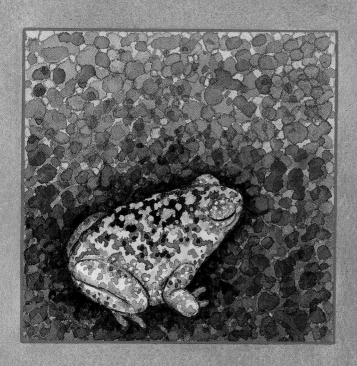

Tap, tap, tap!

Could this be it?

Is this the rain at last?

No, it's a gila woodpecker

tapping

on a tall green cactus.

The toad feels the ground begin to shake.

Then a CRUNCH, CRUNCH, CRUNCH that's loud.

Is this the rain?

No.

It's a park ranger's boots

walking on the path.

What about that *tsk, tsk, tsk*?

Is this the rain at last?

No. It's the rattle of a rattlesnake,

giving warning: **STAY AWAY.**

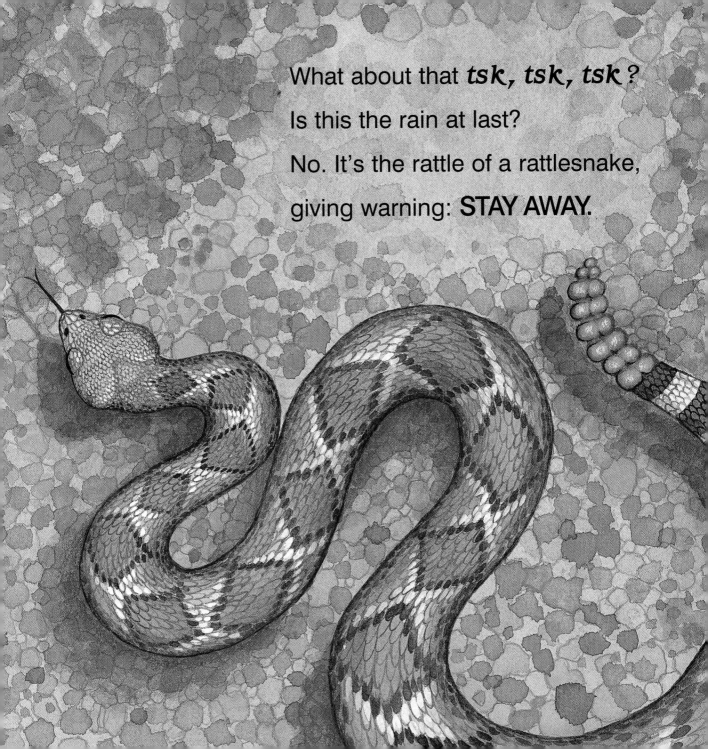

Surely that rumbling . . .

that rumble, rumbling . . . .

Surely that's the rain . . . ?

Not yet.

It's the thunder of a distant storm.

But perhaps the rain is near.

Plip, plop, plip, plop,
plip, plop, plop!

Is this the rain at last?

Plop **thunk.** Plop **thunk.**

Plop **thunk** *gussssshhhhhhh!*

It is rain!

The toad hears it.

She digs.

Plop **thunk,** plop **thunk,** plop **thunk *gussssshhhhhhh***

Heavy rain pounds the desert floor.

Push, push, and the toad pops right out, into the open air.

Bleat, bleat, bleat!

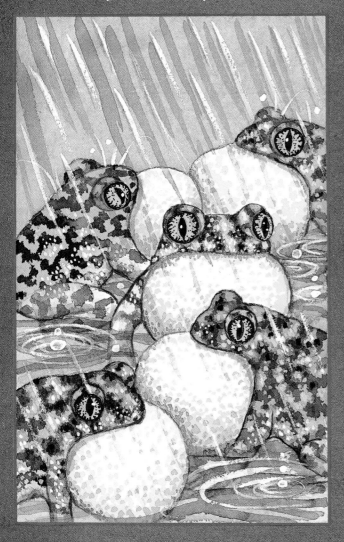

The toad hears loud bleats.

Is that the rain sound too?

No. It's male spadefoot toads, calling: Here, come here!

Come here!

Plop **thunk,** plop **thunk,** plop **thunk** *gussssshhhhhh!*

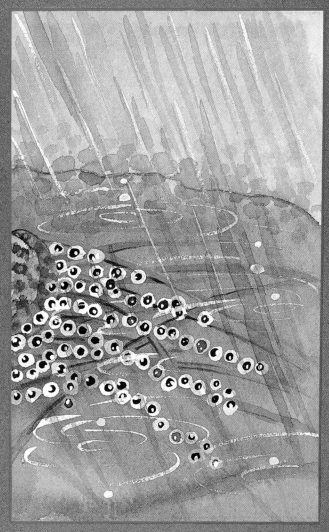

The toad hops in a puddle.

A male rides piggyback.

She lays her eggs,

like beads of glass.

Then the male fertilizes them.

Plop **thunk,** plop **thunk,**

Two days later, the eggs hatch. Wriggling and wiggling

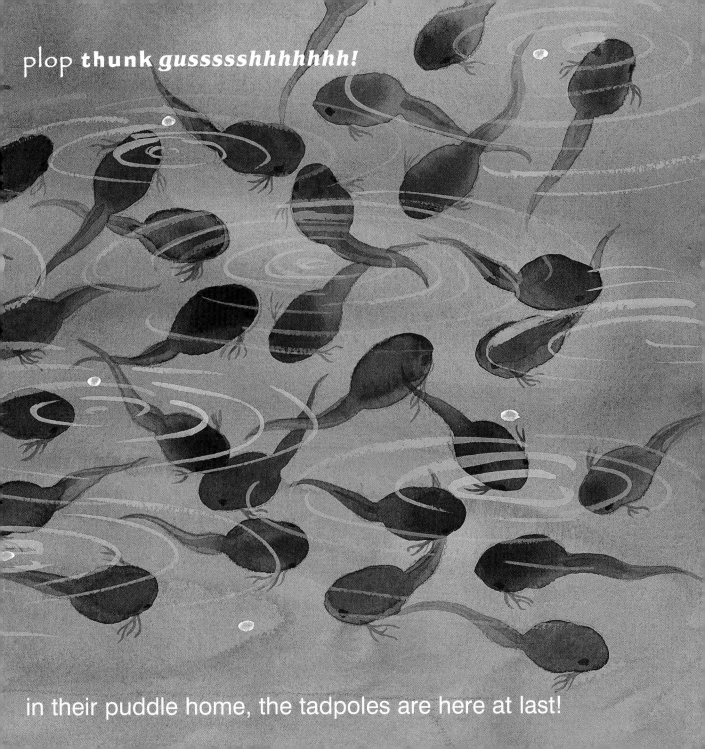

plop **thunk** *gussssshhhhhhh!*

in their puddle home, the tadpoles are here at last!

They eat.

They grow.

Legs start to show.

But their puddle is drying up!

Will any make it?

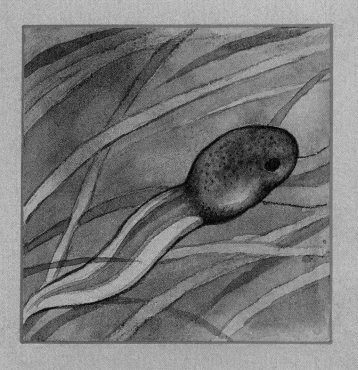

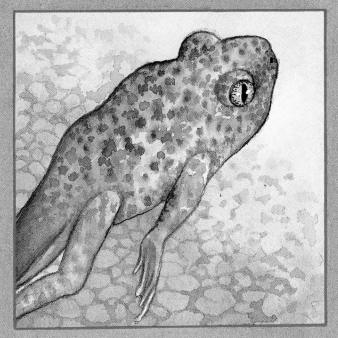

Yes!

With new legs formed,

young toads crawl

from their puddle home.

They rest, then

LEAP

into the desert beyond.

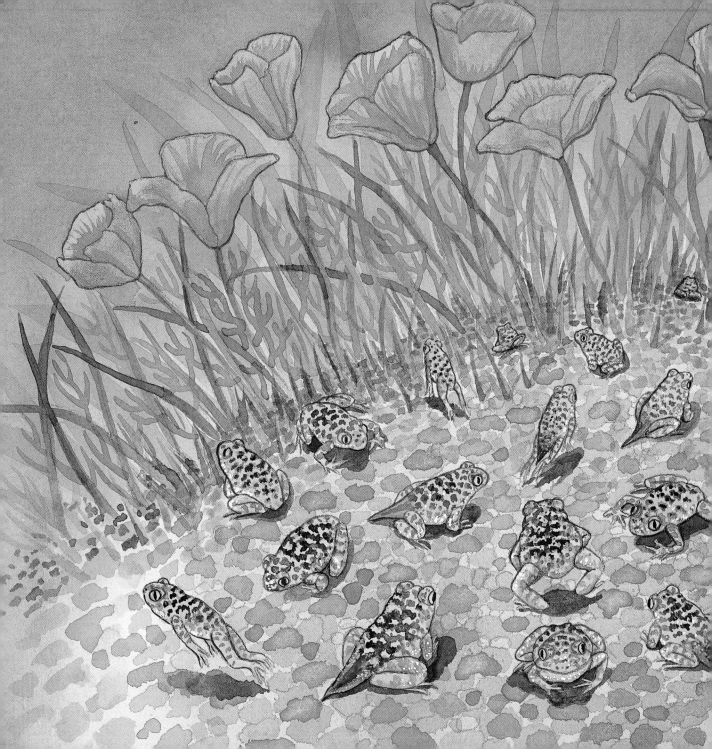

Thump, thump, thump.

Hundreds of tiny toads jump.

The rain has made the desert green.

Yet it won't be long till the desert's dry,

and toads dig down deep

with their spadefoot feet,   to wait for that sound . . .

that marvelous sound,

the sound of the desert rain.

Plop **thunk,** plop **thunk,**

plop **thunk** *gussssshhhhhhh!*

Plop **thunk,** plop **thunk,**

plop **thunk** *gusssssshhhhhhh!*

Plop **thunk,** plop **thunk,**

plop **thunk** *gussssshhhhhhh!*

THE SPADEFOOT TOAD

The Couch's spadefoot toad is found in the desert regions of Texas, California, Arizona, New Mexico, Oklahoma, and Mexico. It is hard for a toad to survive in the desert, yet a Couch's spadefoot toad can. It spends most of the year underground in a cool, moist burrow. This burrow, which it digs with its spadelike feet, may be up to a yard beneath the desert's dry surface.

When a toad hears and feels the vibrations of heavy rainfall, it digs out of its underground home. Male and female spadefoot toads gather in pools and puddles created by the rain. The males call out loudly, sounding a lot like bleating lambs. The toads pair up, with the male riding piggyback on the female. That way, the male will be there when the female lays her eggs in rain pools, and he can fertilize them.

After the eggs are fertilized, the toads hop away to eat their fill of insects. In only two days the eggs hatch. The spadefoot tadpoles eat, grow, and begin to change into toads.

First, back legs form, then front legs. The tadpoles' metamorphosis is quick, taking only two to four weeks. It has to be quick, because desert puddles can dry up rapidly. Not all the tadpoles survive; some are eaten by predators—including other tadpoles.

After the young spadefoot toads leave their puddles, they feed and grow in the desert for a few weeks. Then both the young and adult toads dig back underground to wait until the next heavy rain. It can be a long wait indeed—as long as eleven months—until they hear the rain again.

NOTE: Spadefoot toads belong to their own special scientific family, *Pelobatidae*, because of their spade-shaped feet, relatively smooth skin, and other structural features. This family is closely related to but different from the family *Bufonidae*, the "true toads."

THE SPADEFOOT TOAD'S DESERT NEIGHBORS

1. GIANT DESERT HAIRY SCORPION *(Hadrurus arizonensis)*

These $5\frac{1}{2}$-inch hairy scorpions are some of the largest in the United States. They are active primarily at night, when they hunt and eat insects and occasionally lizards.

2. ORD'S KANGAROO RAT *(Dipodomys ordii)*

Kangaroo rats hop on their hind feet, very much the way kangaroos do. Their bodies are only four inches long, but when chased by predators, kangaroo rats can cover up to six feet in a single leap. These long-tailed rodents scurry about mostly at night, and their diet consists mainly of seeds.

3. COLLARED PECCARY *(Dicotyles tajacu)*

These small, piglike mammals travel in the desert in grunting, squealing herds of ten or twenty and are also called *javelinas*. They eat berries, fruits, seeds, grubs, and even cacti—spines and all!

4. GILA WOODPECKER *(Melanerpes uropygialis)*

A hole in a saguaro cactus is a perfect place for a gila woodpecker to live. Using their sharp beaks, these 10-inch birds excavate holes in the cacti to use as nesting cavities. After a woodpecker abandons a nesting cavity, owls or other birds may move in.

5. WESTERN DIAMONDBACK RATTLESNAKE *(Crotalus atrox)*

These snakes can grow to be over 5 feet long, making them the largest in the western United States. They curl up under rocks or in burrows during the heat of the day, but come out to feed on birds, mice, and rats. The bite of this snake is poisonous and can be lethal to humans.

For my grandfather Thomas F. Richardson,
who taught me that truth has a story too
—A. P. S.

For Wiley, digging deep down in my heart
—B. B.

Special thanks to Craig Ivanyi at the Arizona-Sonora Desert Museum for
his thoughtful review of the manuscript and sketches for this project, as
well as for his help with the art reference research. The illustrator wishes
also to thank C. Allen Morgan for the reference use of his wonderful
photographs of spadefoot tadpole-to-toad transformation.

Library of Congress Cataloging-in-Publication Data
Sayre, April Pulley.
Dig, wait, listen: a desert toad's tale / by April Pulley Sayre ; illustrated by Barbara Bash.
p.   cm.
"Greenwillow Books."
Summary: A spadefoot toad waits under the sand for rain, hears the sounds of
other desert animals, and eventually mates and spawns other toads.
ISBN 0-688-16614-8 (trade). ISBN 0-688-16615-6 (lib. bdg.) 1. Toads—Juvenile fiction.
[1. Toads—Fiction. 2. Desert animals—Fiction.] I. Bash, Barbara, ill. II. Title.
PZ10.3.S277 Di 2001   [E]—dc21   00-032111
First Edition 10 9 8 7 6 5